Tarot Tales

Janani Mohan

BookLeaf
Publishing

India | USA | UK

Tarot Tales © 2023 Janani Mohan

All rights reserved.

No part of this publication may be reproduced, stored in a retrieval system, or transmitted, in any form or by any means, electronic, mechanical, photocopying, recording, or otherwise, without the prior written permission of the presenters.

Janani Mohan asserts the moral right to be identified as the author of this work.

Presentation by *BookLeaf Publishing*

Web: www.bookleafpub.com

E-mail: info@bookleafpub.com

ISBN: 9789357696098

First edition 2023

Dedicated to my parents

ACKNOWLEDGEMENT

To the universe that grants me opportunities to explore the creative realms of my magical existence.

PREFACE

Magic exists in each of our lives. Magic appears as blessings, escapes from dangers as well as opportunities to be a giver of joy. Hope you are blessed with many magical moments as you travel through life.

0 - The Fool

It's begun, the magical journey
I was lost, weak and my mind was stormy,
My wounded heart said, in here, it's thorny,
I needed an escape to a world less rainy.

So it's begun, my magical ride,
Spontaneous calls from my inner child,
I will heed to thee, my wild side,
For your whims and wishes were revealed.

I am ready to take the leap of faith,
For I may fall, I may rise,
My past self floating away like a wraith,
For all I want are less cries and more highs.

Fool, you may call me,
Who thinks not of any consequences,
Fool, I shall be,
For freedom is all I seek.

1 - The Magician

The Agility of Swords,
The Grace of the Cups,
The Abundance of the Pentacles,
The Skill of the Wands,
Have assembled, united as the Four Elements.

All you need is to harness their power,
To unlock your true self,
March on without doubt,
For it is in your soul to weave the magic.

Heed not to the million restrictive thoughts
Let go of all your inhibitions and ego,
Perform your role in this eventful play,
By doing what makes your heartbeat sway.

Do it now, do it with love,
Do it with skill, do with confidence,
Capture this moment of time under your spell,
Captivate the world, for you are the magician.

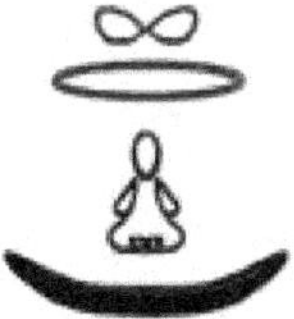

2 - The High Priestess

I hear the inner voice,
More clearly now as I silence the noise,
This voice which guides me,
My mind's eye, my intuition.

Each day we are directed by different voices,
Which questions our identity, our choices,
So many advice, so many opinions,
But as I wind down to bed, I listen to my inner
minion.

Amidst all uncertainties in this realm,
The most powerful soul is the one whose mind is
calm.
When fear, distrust and insecurities make me weak,
I resort to meditation and gain the wisdom I seek.

In the vast ocean of knowledge,
Never shun to break your own boundaries,
Grow every day spiritually and embrace peace,
For you are the High Priestess, trust in thee.

3 - The Empress

In a world full of strong protagonists,
Where the weak are laughed upon,
I challenge thee in the battle of the mind,
For I possess the power of compassion.

Love without any binding,
No expectations, no rewinding,
Being present and one with nature,
Pouring unconditional love onto all living.

I see thy beauty, not in your physical being,
But deep inside thy soul, wherein lies your true
healing,
Surrender thyself to simple living,
For there is meaning in just breathing.

Open your heart to love,
Open your mind to possibilities,
Choose to give and forgive,
For you are the empress in the kingdom of your heart.

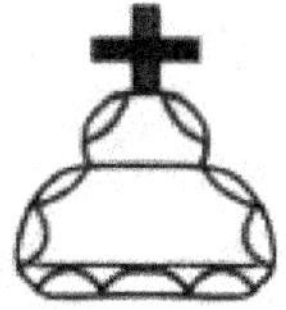

4 - The Emperor

It is the time to act out of valor,
Think head straight,
And use your power to act right,
Since the times are dark.

There are no more black and white,
It's all gray and your senses can be delusional,
It is at this moment you need to stabilize,
And protect your interests at all costs.

Plan ahead in the future,
Keep stock of your mightiest dreams,
Without losing hope in humanity,
Strive to achieve against all odds.

You are born a leader,
You are born with the power to protect humanity,
You are the ruler of your mind,
Think clear and act, for you are the emperor.

5 - The Hierophant

Bravo, you have traveled alone thus far,
A troubled mind, a lost sense of direction,
I sense a need for guidance,
Seek thy mentor, for help shall be given to all who
ask.

I wander about imbibing newly found knowledge,
The one which awakens my soul,
I sense dualities all around me,
For life is not the same as before.

I reprimand myself for the sins of my past,
For I clearly see there is no one right or wrong,
A spiritual cycle has begun now with my priest,
To enlighten in the laps of nature's beast.

I learn about my ancestral roots,
Calming all the unhealed wounds,
For the cycle of unlearning begins,
To rid of the evils that crept in.

6 - The Lovers

Hey companion soul,
How have you been?
I have searched for you far and wide,
Just to meet you in between.

The joy you blossom in my heart,
I return to thee without a thought,
For we are one in every fight,
Together we lift each other with delight.

I take care of you, you take care of mine,
We effortlessly spend our together time,
With millions of differences which make each of us
shine,
I shall always choose you every time.

You are free and so am I,
And together we shall prolong our race,
For lovers we are in every space,
Bonded by trust, love and respect without a chase.

7 - The Chariot

Oh an untamed stallion you were,
Now I see you in control of your mare,
For you have unlocked your willpower,
To channel the positive aura for brighter rides.

Slow and Steady, you ride ahead
Knowing there is a steep learning curve ahead,
You have the perseverance to take the challenge on,
For the faith in yourself is strong.

There are wild thoughts in your mind,
Which aims to pull you down with time,
But you choose to cast them aside,
For all you can see is your growth at sight.

Don't doubt a moment, my brave one,
You shall pass with the gown of colors,
For your purpose is noble and divine,
Upon the chariot you shall ride on.

8 - Strength

Mirror, mirror on the wall,
I am the weakest of them all,
I cried the other night, thinking of the one who broke
my heart,
The pain is ripping me apart.

It's been months now, I touch my heart,
It hurts a bit less, my face shines brighter,
I breathe in and breathe out,
I feel good in my company.

I was bullied as a kid,
I was looked down on as a teenager,
I was laughed at as an adult,
So I decided to dance to my own song.

Mirror, mirror on the wall,
I love myself, unconditionally,
Without any regrets, without any judgements,
I have found the greatest Strength of them all,
self-love.

9 - The Hermit

Winter is here, the perfect time to hibernate,
I lie on my bed, listening to my heartbeat,
Mind creating a line of thoughts to attend to,
But I say no more, I was attending to my soul.

Inside my shell, I retract,
To explore my inner child's desires,
Reconnecting to nature,
Humming songs which makes me happy.

I take out my journal, jot down my dreams,
Best memories of the year,
Helpful lessons though learnt the hard way,
And grateful moments when I felt blessed.

It's the season to be thankful,
Season to look inward and remember the
Little things which made you truly happy,
For your soul deserves to be colorful.

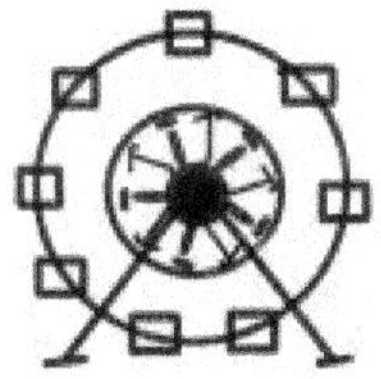

10 - Wheel Of Fortune

The carnival is here,
And yay I want to go up the giant wheel,
To enjoy the ride up and ride down,
With glee and wonder.

Life is but a giant wheel,
We experience happiness, followed by sadness,
Only to meet happiness again,
For there is no light without darkness.

So don't wait for their permission,
Go and do your mission,
Good for all and harm for none,
As these moments are soon gone.

Embrace the rises with humility,
Surrender to the eternal vibration,
Ease into the moments of lows,
Remembering that you are part of this Wheel of
Fortune.

11 - Justice

Inner voice tells me it's not right,
The outer voices applauding me to do it anyway,
It's the battle of conscience,
So who triumphed?

Years later, I sit in the park bench,
Memories floating by as I watch the kids play,
And one more time, I see myself in the little boy,
Perhaps this is my chance to do the right thing now.

Karmic cycles have begun,
You shall seek what thy have sown,
The rewards are doubled for every dime,
The wounds of pain are sharper with time.

Justice is always served hot,
Are you ready to handle its glow?
Whether it burns you or ignites you,
There is no escape from this now.

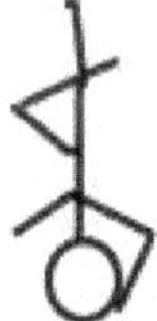

12 - The Hanged Man

We are but puppets in this big cosmic play,
We are too afraid to let go and face isolation,
For we want to be rescued, to be validated,
We believe we are not enough.

As we drive through, most times we run into a cliff,
We hang on its edge, we don't want to take the leap,
We want to hold on to want we hold dear,
We fear the unknown, we fear the fall.

Sometimes, oops, we are forced to take the fall,
For every experience fills up the missing parts of
your soul,
The stillness on the clifftop, makes you realize,
That the unknown abyss might be your only chance.

Simply let go, surrender to the universe,
Learn and elevate yourself,
It's never going to be easy,
But it is definitely going to be worth it.

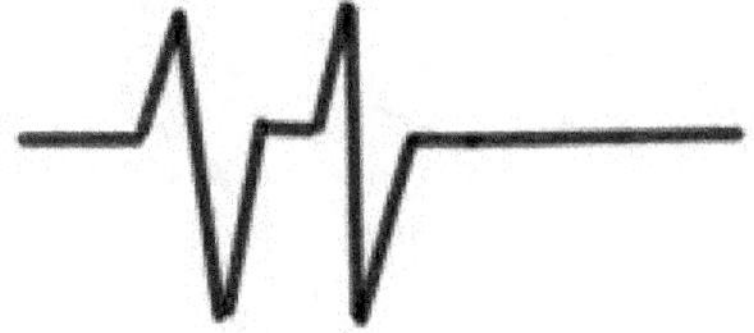

13 - Death

A thousand deaths in my lifetime, a wise man said,
I died many times to rediscover myself,
A more aligned self, more peaceful self,
Less didactic, less rigid.

I need to shed this skin, it's too heavy now,
Too wriggled with constrained thoughts,
For I was taught there is only one right way,
But life opened a door to infinite possibilities.

I have to cast away this burdened self,
And embrace the new dimensions of life,
I feel the pain of change, for it takes away
People and things you hold dear.

This transformation is a must,
For it brings you a closure which is just,
For after Death comes rebirth,
Which restores the balance the mind sought.

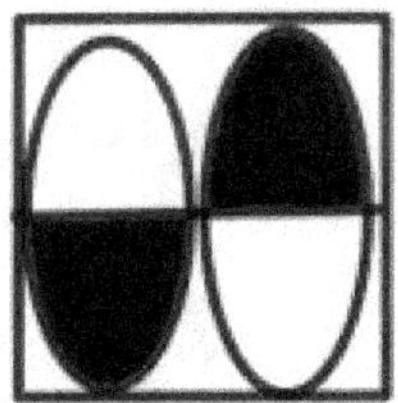

14 - Temperance

Some days my heart yearns for something, Which
clearly my mind condemns,
May be there is a way to balance between the two,
A middle path which can make them both happy.

Middle paths are tricky,
You would be labeled as tactful, cunning
And at times even called as the chameleon,
The hardest part is you then become picky.

Moderation is hard to adopt,
Even harder to stick to,
You will be enticed by both sides of this black and
white world,
At those times, remember you are the colorful
rainbow.

Choose your balance at this moment,
Choose the vibrations with the now you,
Be open to cognitive dissonances,
Choose harmony and put your ego to rest.

15 - The Devil

I feel a brooding storm of darkness,
Lingering in my shadows,
But all l see is you before me,
As a pompous sensual rose in a glass jar.

I see all your red thorns, the promises you failed to keep,
The pangs of loneliness I felt when we were in a crowd,
But you are my drug, all I needed is the reassuring smile
In your shining face to pull me right back to you.

My shadow is pleading from behind,
Warning me of your deceitful gaze,
My dreams remind me of my addictive ways,
Until the day your smiles fade and you throw me away.

It was just like a fairytale, which turned into a nightmare,
For somewhere in between the pixie dust and starry nights,
I allowed you to overpower me, to control my mind,
Become the possessive devil of my life.

16 - The Tower

I wake up in the middle of the night,
And ask myself, Who am I ?
2 am identity crisis is real deal,
I am covered with the dust of my dilapidated self.

I am not able to attach to the past me,
I am drowned in shame, guilt and remorse,
Of all the choices I made, of all the hate speeches
I inflicted on myself, all the broken pieces around
me.

Tears are rolling down my cheek,
Rage is brooding through my veins,
For I chose to expose my insecurities,
I chose to paint myself green.

 It is an upheaval, washing away my perceived
constants,
All my defenses are crumbling down,
I don't recognize myself anymore,
I am falling off this tower of identity.

17 - The Star

It is pitch dark outside my camping tent,
Up above, the twinkle of millions of stars waits to
surprise me,
Much like the little gifts hidden in my soul,
Waiting to be revealed to this universe.

A sense of hope, of warmth fills my heart,
I realize my untapped potential,
Hidden in my infectious laughter, in my emphatic
hug,
In my applauding cheer and altruistic attitude.

In this world of trillions of inhabitants,
We are all a speckled wonder,
Filled with the energy of the star,
To boundlessly dazzle in our own form.

Born from the same everlasting flame,
We share the inherent glow which shines brighter,
When lit by unconditional love,
For we are all here to shine in the colors of our soul.

18 - The Moon

I roamed around aimlessly in my subconscious mind,
Seeking clarity in this world of chaos,
I feel something is not right,
Things are not what they seem.

Questions arise out of nowhere,
In my otherwise calm mind,
What is real, what is dreamy,
Is still unclear.

Trust is a bridge we build with our dear ones,
Brick by brick, we open our heart to them,
Soon to realize it was a bridge to nowhere,
When the fog of illusion lifts off.

Beware my friend, all that glitters is not gold,
Wait for clarity before you reveal your soul,
Impatience is not the meaning of bold,
Break those fears to become whole.

19 - The Sun

Happiness is best when shared,
I realized that when someone cared,
For a simple smile is all you need,
To make someone's day brighter indeed.

Success fills you with joy and ecstasy,
Your confidence is boosted,
Your clarity is enhanced,
And you spread radiance as you speak.

Your heart is light and body is bright,
You see the world in golden light,
It is your time to shine,
Helping others to see the divine.

Experience the bundle of abundance,
And even greater joy of sharing it with all,
For the brighter you glow, when you share your light,
Like the ever vibrant Sun, which sets at night.

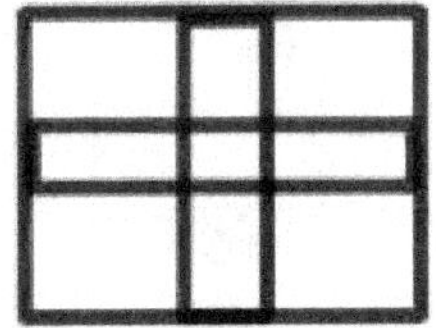

20 - Judgement

Oh I have been deceived by thee,
Even when I shared your burdens with glee,
Soon I have a heavy heart,
With all the blame on my part.

Jaded I was in the past,
Emotionally involved and lost,
For now I choose to let it go,
Forgiving is good for my soul.

To accept reality as it is,
Not clouding it with a fairytale bliss,
Is a lesson we all must learn,
To gain the peace we all yearn.

The Judgement Day is here,
Discard all of your fear,
Embrace the beauty of your present life,
Expand your wings and get rid of the strife.

21 - The World

Here I am at the end of a cycle,
Looking back at the journey to completion,
I feel united to my true self,
A beatific smile spreads across my face.

The ups and downs make more sense,
The blessings and lessons complete me in all sense,
I feel whole once again,
Ready to take on challenges without constraint.

I am connected to all that is divine,
I feel thy hands in mine,
I take a moment to rejoice this time,
Opening my heart to the next in line.

Always believe in your silly dreams,
For they have the power to create magical beams,
Be grateful in your prime,
The World is within your reach all the time.

www.ingramcontent.com/pod-product-compliance
Lightning Source LLC
LaVergne TN
LVHW021353200726

843509LV00014B/2825